INFORMATION EXPLORER

SUPER SMART
INFORMATION
STRATEGIES

SHOOTING
VIDEO TO MAKE
LEARNING FUN

by Julie Green

CHERRY LAKE PUBLISHING • ANN ARBOR, MICHIGAN

A NOTE TO PARENTS AND TEACHERS: Please remind your children how to stay safe online before they do the activities in this book.

A NOTE TO KIDS: Always remember your safety comes first!

Published in the United States of America
by Cherry Lake Publishing
Ann Arbor, Michigan
www.cherrylakepublishing.com

Content Adviser: Gail Dickinson, PhD,
Associate Professor, Old Dominion University,
Norfolk, Virginia

Book design and illustration: The Design Lab

Photo credits: Cover, ©iStockphoto.com/FineCollection; page 4, ©iStockphoto.
com/track5; page 6, ©iStockphoto.com/LUGO; page 10, ©Rick Becker-
Leckrone/Shutterstock, Inc.; page 11, ©Inspirestock Inc./Alamy; page
13, ©iStockphoto.com/lovleah; page 15, ©bikeriderlondon/Shutterstock,
Inc.; page 18, ©Condor 36/Shutterstock, Inc.; page 22, ©Rob Marmion/
Shutterstock, Inc.; page 25, ©iStockphoto.com/digitalskillet; page 27,
©NetPhotos/Alamy; page 29, ©Kuttig-Travel-2/Alamy

Library of Congress Cataloging-in-Publication Data
Green, Julie, 1982–
    Super smart information strategies. Shooting video to make learning fun/
by Julie Green.
        p. cm.—(Information explorer)
    Includes bibliographical references and index.
    ISBN-13: 978-1-60279-955-4 (lib. bdg.)
    ISBN-10: 1-60279-955-5 (lib. bdg.)
    1. Digital cinematography—Juvenile literature. 2. Internet
videos—Juvenile literature. 3. Motion pictures—Production and
direction—Juvenile literature. I. Title. II. Title: Shooting video to
inform and entertain. III. Series.
    TR860.G74 2010
    778.5'30285—dc22   2010002022

Cherry Lake Publishing would like to acknowledge the work
of The Partnership for 21st Century Skills. Please visit
www.21stcenturyskills.org for more information.

Printed in the United States of America
Corporate Graphics Inc.
July 2010
CLFA07

Table of Contents

CHAPTER ONE

Planning Your Movie

What kinds of movies does your family like to watch?

Do you like watching movies? There are so many fantastic options to choose from. Sure, movies entertain us. But they can also teach us a lot about different people, places, and times. Films are great learning tools. In this book, we'll learn how movies you make yourself can make projects interesting. So get ready. It's time to put your skills as a movie planner, actor, and director to the test!

Think about all of the movies you have seen in your life. There are many different kinds of movies that tell many different stories. Deep down, movies are simply stories told using video. Can you write or tell a story? You can also make a movie, but it will take some planning to make it go smoothly from start to finish.

First, you must organize your thoughts. Try writing down all of your ideas using a list or graphic organizer. This will help you figure out what you want the

Happiness
Love
Baseball
Strangers

Monsters
Action
Adventure

Animation
Ghosts
Evil
Haunted

You can combine ideas from two of your favorite movies using a graphic organizer.

5

subject of the film to be. You might have a great idea. If you aren't ready to shoot it, you can save it for later. In time, you will probably decide how to move forward with it.

Sometimes, your own experiences are the best material for a movie. Maybe you went on a great vacation or had an interesting bus ride home from school one day. These stories could make wonderful movies! Making a movie of something that happened in your own life is a nice place to start. Why? You already went through the experience. You know exactly what happened and how you felt.

Your movie does not need to be a full-length Hollywood production. Films for school assignments are often just a few minutes long.

Your trip to an amusement park might be a good subject for a movie.

Maybe one of your favorite memories is making Christmas cookies with your grandmother.

Movies can also be informational. How could you teach your audience about what everyday life was like years ago? Maybe you could film an interview of your grandmother talking about her childhood. Movies don't have to be huge, complicated creations. They just have to be interesting and original.

Have you chosen an idea for a story? Write it down. You can do this in any way that works for you. You may want to create an outline, use a graphic organizer, or write a script. Plan out the beginning, middle, and end of your movie. Then think carefully about how each of those parts is going to look, feel, and sound. Do you have an idea and a plan for how to show that idea? Then you are almost ready to start filming!

TRY THIS!

Imagine your class is learning about nutrition. Your teacher has assigned you to create a television-style cooking segment. It should be a few minutes long. With a partner, you must show how to make a simple, healthy snack. A storyboard is one way to plan out your ideas. Storyboards are a series of boxes that show the order of the action in a film. Each box has a sketch of the action for one camera setup.

Make a storyboard with a friend. Need a recipe idea? How about trail mix? Look online for a recipe if you're not sure how to make it. Draw a picture in each box of the storyboard showing the different scenes of your cooking segment. Then write a sentence or two beneath each box. Explain what is happening in that scene. Also, jot down a line or two of what you will say in the film. Use as many boxes as you need.

continued ⟶

Once you have finished, show your storyboard to a family member. Have your family member try to explain the process you are showing. If he or she can explain it, then you know you have done a good job of planning your shots. If you are planning to film a story, the person should be able to tell you the beginning, middle, and end. Do you have to explain the entire clip? If so, go back and add more details. Careful planning will make your films a success.

Shot of all the ingredients

Show how to mix everything

End with close-up of trail mix

CHAPTER TWO
Thinking About Shots

Choose shots that will give your audience the best view of the action.

Do you think a video clip would be interesting if the camera never moved? There might be times when a single camera shot works for a scene, but a variety of shots is often more interesting.

You should think about what kinds of shots you would like to include in your video clips. Different shots have different effects. A long shot shows a person's entire body. These shots help introduce a person to the audience. A medium shot is closer. It shows a person from the waist up. Close-ups feature an actor's face and shoulders. They really show a person's emotions.

You should also experiment with different camera angles. Film your subject from the front, side, or even from above. See which angles work best. Try zooming in or out. Think carefully about your shots. They have a big effect on how well you share the story or message of your video.

Close-ups can help draw the audience into your movie.

TRY THIS!

Watch a cooking show on television to get ideas for interesting shots. There's a good chance you'll see close-ups of ingredients. You might also see close-ups of the chef's hands as she works. Are there any medium or long shots? Do you notice any interesting camera angles?

Now revisit your cooking segment storyboard with your partner. What type of shot would be best for each box? Write the name of that shot beneath each box next to your other notes. Redraw your sketches or add more boxes to reflect these shots if necessary. Do you see how different shots can improve your video clip?

Try some close-ups

CHAPTER THREE
Shooting Your Movie

What kind of equipment will you use to record your movie?

You know what you're going to film. You have a storyboard. Now, you need to decide what kind of camera you're going to use. There are many different kinds. Pick the one that's right for you. You might be able to record video using things you already have in your home. These include cell phones and digital cameras. Have you decided to use either of these to shoot video?

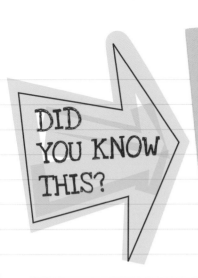

DID
YOU KNOW
THIS?

Different cameras
and video devices have
different features
and video quality. Test
different models before
choosing the one that's
best for you.

Many cameras allow you to quickly record videos and transfer them to your computer. Some camcorders can be connected to computers with USB cables. Then the video files can be transferred to the computer.

Think about where you want to film your scenes. Dark rooms will make it difficult to see anything. Too many shadows can also affect the picture.

Think about the background of your shots, too. Is it too dull? Is it so busy that it distracts your viewers? You want to make sure the background and lighting add to your movie.

Audio, or sound, is also important. You want your viewers to be able to clearly hear everything. Imagine filming on a busy street. There would probably be too much background noise from horns honking or the wind blowing. A quiet space may be best for filming. That way, your viewers will be able to hear whoever is speaking. Do you have access to an extra microphone? It may help you pick up sounds without having to make people speak louder.

As you film, do not be afraid to redo your shots. Even famous directors record parts of their movies over and over again. Watch your footage. Pay attention to the background, the sound, and the lighting. It is also a good idea to show the video to other people you're working with. Others might notice sound or lighting problems that you missed. Work together. Talk about ways to improve the clips.

Once you have filmed your video, you'll need to transfer the file to a computer. Make sure you save your movie files in a place where they won't accidentally get deleted. Give your files specific names so you can tell them apart.

Most video cameras let you play back your footage to see if you need to redo a shot.

TRY THIS!

Ask an adult if you can borrow a camcorder or other video recording device. You may also be able to use one from school. Ask a teacher or media center worker. Take some time to get familiar with the features of whatever device you'll be using. Practice filming something or someone. If you are trying out different models, shoot test clips that are 10 to 30 seconds long. That way, you can really pay attention to whether or not you like that kind of recorder.

Once you've decided on a recording device, shoot another clip. You can shoot the cooking segment you planned earlier. One person should shoot the segment. Another person should demonstrate the recipe. When you are finished, the two of you can switch roles and shoot the segment again.

continued ⟶

continued ⟶

You can also make a fresh storyboard about another topic of your choice and shoot it. Use your storyboard as a guide as you frame your shots. Pay attention to sound and lighting in your scenes. Transfer and save the video files to a computer when you're done. Ask an adult for help if you need it.

There is a stranger in the front of the house.

The stranger gets out of the car.

Run for your life!

The stranger meant no harm.

ARE YOU REALLY AFRAID?

Try drawing a new storyboard. Remember to pay attention to camera angles, lighting, and sound.

CHAPTER FOUR
Editing Your Movie

You've shot your movie and saved it on a computer.
Does that mean you're done? Not yet! Stopping at this
point would be like baking a cake and forgetting to frost
it. It's time to edit your movie and add some fun extras.
To do this, you will need to use computer software.

There are many different kinds of editing software.
Using what works for you—and what you may already

⌐ Editing is one of the most important parts of
making a movie.

18

have—is the best idea. Two popular kinds of editing software are Windows Movie Maker and iMovie.

Editing a movie can take a few minutes, or it can take many hours. It all depends on what you want to do and your attention to detail. Editing software allows you to cut out parts of your movie. Have you ever heard of outtakes? They are shots that are not included in the final edit of a film. Maybe the actors forgot their lines and are laughing. The film editors will cut out those parts. You can do the same thing with your own footage. For example, maybe your hand was shaky when holding the camera. Edit that part from your movie. Follow your software's directions to trim clips.

With editing software, you can also add a title to the beginning of your movie and credits at the end. Some programs allow you to add cool effects such as background music.

If you add music to your movie, make sure you have legal permission to use it. There are also some great online sites that offer copyright-free music you can download. Ask an adult to help you find one.

It is a lot of fun to test how different effects change the look and feel of your video. Make sure, however, that any effects do not overshadow the main ideas of your movie. Did viewers pay more attention to the glittery words dancing across the screen than what happened in your clip? Then you have some reworking to do. Make sure any extras support, rather than distract from, your message.

TRY THIS!

Put your editing skills to the test. Make a 30-second movie tour of a room in your house. Then ask an adult if you can use a computer with editing software. Play around with the software and edit your clip. Add all of the extras and effects you can, even if the final product looks out of control. Then make a second movie tour of another room in your house. This time, edit more carefully. Only add a few effects. These may include a title, end credits, or soft background music.

continued ⟶

continued ———→

Compare the two videos. Show them to a friend. Discuss the strengths and weaknesses of each clip. Do you see how important it is to edit your shots with a careful hand?

Now go back and edit the clips you shot for the activity in Chapter 3. Remember: Edit thoughtfully!

Try all the different ways to transition between shots.

Once you have cut and tweaked your video, save the edited file. Your project is now complete!

CHAPTER FIVE
Sharing Your Movie

One of the simplest ways to share your video is to play it back on your computer.

Think about all of the ways to watch videos using your computer. You can insert a DVD and use your computer monitor like a television screen. With the help of an adult, you can go online and watch videos people have posted. You can visit the Web site of a television show and watch an episode.

With a little help, you can use different options to share your own videos. It's time to show off your clips. You have worked hard and deserve to share your project with your fans!

One way to share your video file is to simply show others from your computer. You could also save the movie to a CD, DVD, or flash drive. Then you could watch the video on a friend's computer. Another way to share your video is to upload it to a portable device, such as an iPod or a laptop.

Do you have grandparents or friends that live very far away? Showing them your videos in person may not be possible. You still want to show off those videos, though. So how can you solve this problem? Look no further than the Internet. There are many quick and easy ways to share videos through certain Web sites.

Flash drives and DVDs are two ways to save and share your videos.

If you decide to share videos online, you must be very careful. Any personal information should not be shared with anyone you do not know. Personal information is anything that could let a stranger figure out who you are. Your phone number, last name, address, and the name of your school are examples of personal information. You wouldn't want to put the movie tours of your home that you created in the last activity online.

Work with your teacher or an adult family member when using the Internet. Not everyone who is online is friendly. You want to make sure you are being as safe as you can.

Always keep safety in mind when you use the Internet!

PERSONAL INFORMATION

One way you can use the Internet to share your video with others is through e-mail. As long as your video file is small enough, you can attach it to an e-mail. Then you can send it to friends and family members who have e-mail accounts. Your editing software may have an option for sending your files through e-mail. If so, it may automatically shrink the file size for you.

When e-mailing videos to close friends and family members, you can be pretty sure that you can trust your audience, but you also have to remember that they can forward your e-mail to others. For this reason, make sure you wouldn't mind other people seeing your movie.

Ask a parent to watch your videos and help you make sure it is safe to e-mail them to other people.

Are you trying to decide the best way to share your videos? Think about the pros and cons of different options. For example, you can quickly send video files to others through e-mail, but the quality of the picture might not be as good as files saved to CDs or DVDs. Which choice would be best for your project needs? Think about it. Make a thoughtful, informed decision. That's what expert information explorers do!

Another option is to transfer your video to the Internet. Your parents might have a blog that they can post your video to. Your teacher might have a wiki to which you can post videos and other projects. A wiki is a special Web site. More than one person can edit and add to the site. You haven't heard of wikis or blogs before? Ask your teacher about them. There are some free blog and wiki sites that your teacher can sign up for if he or she hasn't already.

Working with others can make your videos even better. A classroom wiki is great, because you can post your video. Then your classmates can watch the clip and comment on it. They can type comments about what they like about your video. They can also give you tips for how to improve your skills for next time. Do you see how feedback can make you a better moviemaker?

You can also post your video to an online sharing site. Some include YouTube (*www.youtube.com*) and

Videos posted on YouTube can be viewed by people around the world.

Facebook (*www.facebook.com*). These sites require you to be 13 years old or older. If you decide to share your video using these sites, you will need an adult's help and permission. The adult will have to post the file to a site where he or she has an account.

These sharing sites can make it possible for anyone to find and view your video. An adult can help you with privacy protection. Protecting your video lets you decide who can watch it. That can mean the whole Internet world, or just the people you invite. Many video sharers have found large audiences using these sites, but you must remember that your audience may include people you don't know. Be very careful, and always work with a responsible adult.

TRY THIS!

E-mail a finished video to one friend or family member. Ask him or her to watch the clip. Then the person should e-mail you back with any tips or comments on your work. Repeat this process with another friend or family member. Did you receive the same kinds of comments from both people? How was the feedback different? Think about how you could apply those comments to improve your video.

Then ask a teacher or adult family member to help you share your video online. One option is to use a wiki. Making videos is fun. But proudly sharing your work with others is exciting, too!

Your family is sure to be impressed with your new movie.

Shooting video lets you get creative with your projects. Can you think of more fun clips to make? You could create a news broadcast. You could demonstrate a cultural dance. The important thing to remember when shooting videos is to use tools that work for you. Develop exciting ideas and stay organized. Stay safe online. Be proud of your creations, but stay open to the ideas and help of others at the same time.

Hollywood big shots aren't the only ones who can make movies, information explorer. You can create your very own if you put your mind to it. Ready? Lights! Camera! Action!

What kind of movie will you shoot next?

Glossary

blog (BLAWG) a personal, online journal with entries from its author

feedback (FEED-bak) reactions to something or comments about something

flash drive (FLASH DRIVE) a small, portable storage device used to save files and information

graphic organizer (GRAF-ik OR-guh-nye-zur) a visual representation that helps organize information and show relationships between ideas

outtakes (OUT-tayks) shots that are edited out of a movie's final cut

personal information (PUR-suh-nuhl in-for-MAY-shuhn) information that identifies you, including your name, age, and address

posted (POHST-id) published work or messages on a wiki, blog, or other online setup

USB (yoo-ess-BEE) a type of connection for attaching specific devices to computers

wiki (WI-kee) a Web site that allows users to add and edit content and information

Find Out More

BOOKS

Dunn, Mary R. *I Want to Make Movies*. New York: PowerKids Press, 2009.

Jakubiak, David J. *A Smart Kid's Guide to Avoiding Online Predators*. New York: PowerKids Press, 2010.

Mack, Jim. *Journals and Blogging*. Chicago: Heinemann-Raintree, 2009.

WEB SITES

KidsHealth—Your Online Identity

kidshealth.org/kid/watch/house/online_id.html

Read tips for staying safe online.

Windows Movie Maker How-To Center

www.microsoft.com/windowsxp/using/moviemaker/default.mspx

Find out more about using one type of editing software.

Index

About the Author

Julie Green is a school librarian in Michigan. She loves living her dream of connecting kids to literature!